Dutch Treat

196 Appliqué Blocks Inspired by Delft Designs

JUDY GARDEN

Martingale®
& COMPANY

DEDICATION

For Geoff.
My love, for always.

ACKNOWLEDGMENTS

THERE ARE always people without whose influence and support major projects would never get off the ground. This book is no exception.

I would like to thank my very dear friend Jill Pettit. Working in her wonderful store, Jillybean's Pride, in Oakville, Ontario, set me on my path to quilt creativity. Without Jill's support and unflagging encouragement, this book would not have been written.

My thanks also to the Goodwives Quilters of Darien, Connecticut, who changed me from a machine appliquér into a lover of handwork. Their support and enthusiasm kept me going when the number of blocks I had set as my goal threatened to overwhelm me.

And finally, I want to thank my husband, Geoff, for his love and support. His encouragement and faith in me turned this book from an idea into reality.

CREDITS

President • *Nancy J. Martin*
CEO • *Daniel J. Martin*
Publisher • *Jane Hamada*
Editorial Director • *Mary V. Green*
Managing Editor • *Tina Cook*
Technical Editor • *Jane Townswick*
Copy Editor • *Mary R. Martin*
Design Director • *Stan Green*
Illustrator • *Laurel Strand*
Cover Designer • *Regina Girard*
Text Designer • *Trina Stahl*
Photographer • *Brent Kane*

Martingale®
& COMPANY

That Patchwork Place®

That Patchwork Place® is an imprint of
Martingale & Company®.

Dutch Treat: 196 Appliqué Blocks Inspired by Delft Designs
© 2004 by Judy Garden

Martingale & Company
20205 144th Avenue NE
Woodinville, WA 98072-8478 USA
www.martingale-pub.com

Printed in China
09 08 07 06 05 04   8 7 6 5 4 3 2 1

MISSION STATEMENT
Dedicated to providing quality products and service to inspire creativity.

Library of Congress Cataloging-in-Publication Data

Garden, Judy.
    Dutch treat : 196 appliqué blocks inspired by Delft designs / Judy Garden.
        p. cm.
    ISBN 1-56477-526-7
1. Appliqué—Patterns. 2. Patchwork—Patterns. 3. Blue in interior decoration. 4. White in interior decoration. I. Title.
    TT779.G37 2004
    746.46—dc22
                                                    2003027005

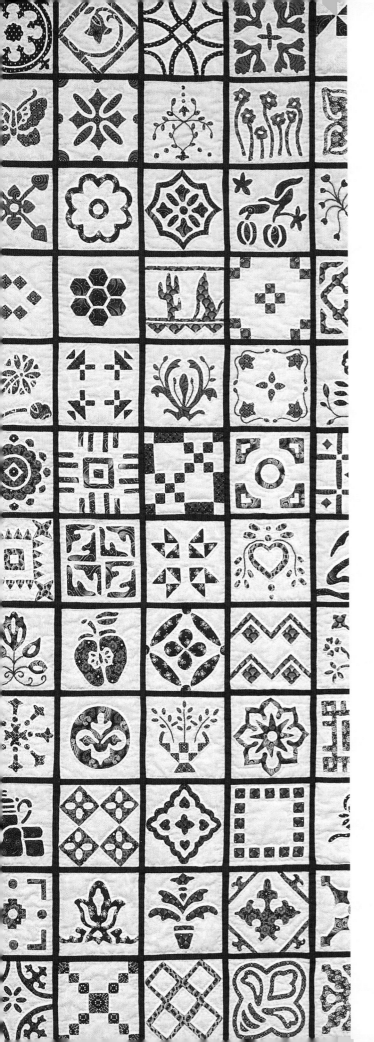

Contents

Deft Delft *by Judy Garden, Connecticut, 71" x 71", 2003.*

The Story Behind the "Deft Delft" Quilt

I HAVE ALWAYS been a collector, and my husband's career in banking has allowed me to live in interesting places around the world and create wonderful collections. When we lived in California, my passion was Father Christmas figures. When we lived in England a few years ago, I thought it would be a very English thing to collect novelty teapots, especially as my husband and I were avid tea drinkers. I discovered quickly, however, that the price of a single teapot would feed my family of five for three days. Needless to say, I did not start that collection!

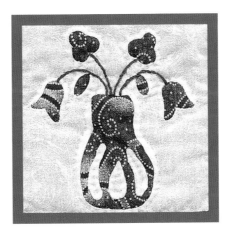

Later, however, when we spent a day at Greenwich Market, I fell in love with a set of six blue-and-white bread-and-butter plates. The price for these plates was the equivalent of ice cream cones all around, so I knew that my next collection was about to begin. Those first little plates looked lonely on the plate rail in our dining room, but they were soon joined by other flea market finds. England is a gold mine for blue-and-white china, and there wasn't a market or antique shop anywhere that didn't have a plate or a bowl to offer at an affordable price of a dollar or two.

One of our moves within England resulted in a substantial insurance claim. During the unpacking process, we found lampshades accordioned into flat disks, broken bed frames, and boxes filled with unrecognizable bits and pieces that had once been whole items. The insurance check we received covered the replacement costs of the damaged items, with a bit left over. We used the extra money to buy a pine Welsh dresser to hold my growing collection of blue-and-white china.

My love for blue and white didn't stop at china, however; delft blue plates and bowls had only paved the way for blue-and-white tiles. During our travels in England, we spent many wonderful hours wandering throughout old churches, castles, and stately homes. We discovered spectacular tiles in hallways and kitchen areas, and most of the old homes we visited had wonderful and extensive col-lections of delft china, Chinese porcelains, and Italian tile work. The endless variety of designs on both china and tiles appealed to me tremendously, and I had long wanted to make a quilt designed around blue-and-white tiles.

Soon afterward, in a hunt for drapery fabric for our living room, I discovered a book called *Blue and White Living* by Stephanie Hoppen. This was definitely "me"! Drapery fabric was forgotten as I brought home my new treasure. Every page of that book showed amazing photographs of blue-and-white china, tiles, ceramics, and fabrics. The pages I kept returning to were the ones that featured small tiles lining bathroom walls and kitchen backsplashes. The quilt of blue and white I had wanted to make for so long suddenly seemed something I had to do.

I always keep a good supply of graph paper and pencils in my quilting studio, and before that afternoon was over, I had drawn dozens of designs for a blue-and-white quilt. Those first designs simply flowed from my pencil. I couldn't wait to get started on actually sewing them!

I began translating my drawings to fabric, and whenever I ran out of designs, I went back to the drafting table to create more. I did research at kitchen design stores and local bookstores, and discovered that even books on my own shelves contained ideas for designs that translated well to

4" blocks. The incredible variety of ceramic designs surrounding us everywhere continues to amaze me.

Eventually, I decided that if I ever wanted to actually finish my quilt, I would have to stop designing and start putting it together. By this time, I had stitched 196 blocks.

Now, what surprises me the most after having made my "Deft Delft" quilt is that more and more ideas continue to come to me. I can think of all kinds of wonderful projects to make using the tile designs in this book.

I hope you will enjoy both the "Deft Delft" quilt and the limitless possibilities open to you when you use the tile designs.

A Quilter's Tools

❈

THE FOLLOWING LIST contains my particular favorites when it comes to tools of the trade. Experiment with any that you have not tried and see if you like them as much as I do.

Rotary cutter, mat, and rulers: These are self-explanatory, and I don't know many quilters who work without them. One tool that is especially nice to have for the blocks in this book is a 4½"-square acrylic ruler.

Mechanical pencil: For tracing patterns onto fabric, I use a mechanical pencil that has a hard, very fine lead and draws a consistently fine line.

Eraser: A good way to remove light pencil markings from fabric is to use a fabric eraser. Find these at your local quilt shop or art supply store.

Needles: For appliquéing blocks, I like to use a size #11 Sharp. It is sharp, thin, and just the right length for tucking under the fabric. For embroidery, I use an embroidery needle that has an eye large enough to accommodate two strands of floss.

Needle threader: A needle threader is indispensable for guiding fine thread through the narrow opening in a size #11 Sharp needle.

Thimble: A thimble protects the finger I use to push the needle. Explore the variety of thimbles available. Look for one that feels so comfortable that you hardly know you're wearing it.

Thread: I find that 60-weight, 100%-cotton machine embroidery thread is a very fine thread that leaves a barely noticeable stitch. Match the thread you choose for recessed appliqué as closely as possible to your foreground fabric. You also will need a spool of regular sewing thread for basting the foreground and main-print fabrics together before you begin to stitch.

Scissors: A very small, sharp pair of scissors is essential for appliqué. Check carefully to make sure that your scissors cut all the way to the point with precision. Many small scissors "grab" the fabric *before* they cut it, which causes the fabric to ravel and leaves an uneven cut. Once you find that perfect pair of scissors, protect it at all costs.

Tracing paper: Tracing paper is available in rolls at any good art supply store. It is invaluable for tracing patterns, especially borders. It is much easier to work with one long segment of paper than to match and tape several sheets together.

Permanent marker: Use a very fine-point permanent marker to trace a design onto tracing paper. Permanent ink is easier to see through fabric than pencil lines, and it will not rub off on fabric the way graphite does.

Painter's tape: This tape helps hold fabric to the book when you are marking designs, and it is easy to remove without damaging the book or leaving adhesive residue on your fabric.

Walking foot: I insert a walking foot in my sewing machine when I assemble a quilt top. This presser foot moves with the action of the feed dogs, rather than against them, so that both layers of fabric move through the machine evenly.

Light table: A light table is optional, but it is helpful if your choice of foreground fabric(s) is something other than white. If you do not have a light table, tape the patterns and fabrics to a window and trace them.

Choosing Fabrics

I WANTED MY "Deft Delft" quilt to be a study in blue and white. I found some wonderful indigo-dyed fabrics at the Quilter's Heritage Show in Lancaster, Pennsylvania, when I visited Sandra McCay's "Cotton in the Cabin" booth (see "Resources," page 126). I chose approximately 14 different prints of the same indigo blue to use as the main print in my quilt. This is the lower layer of fabric that creates the actual design of the quilt.

For the foreground fabric, or upper layer, I chose a variety of white tone-on-tone prints. You can follow the approach I took or let your own creativity lead you to other color combinations. This quilt would look equally beautiful with all-red or all-green fabrics as the main print and one or more whites as the foreground fabric. Another idea would be to use many different colors of fabric for the main print, with one or more whites as the foreground fabric. You might also explore the possibility of using a dark foreground fabric, and letting the main print be either a single contrast print or a selection of different prints. The possibilities are almost endless!

Normally in recessed appliqué, the areas of underlying print that do not show in the final work are cut away from the back side after the stitching is completed. This eliminates the bulk of an extra layer. However, I left both layers of fabric intact in my blocks. I did this because some of the designs required more of the underlying main print to be cut away than others did. If I'd trimmed the background print, the foreground fabric in some blocks would have looked brighter than others. As a result, the eye would have been drawn to the brighter whites. I decided that the subtle shading of the blue main prints showing through the white foreground fabrics would make my entire quilt background uniform in value. I also layered a main-print fabric underneath the white 1" border and treated both fabrics as one for the same reason, even though there is no appliqué in that border.

As you choose fabrics for your quilt, keep in mind whether you want to quilt by hand or by machine. Because recessed appliqué is handwork, I felt it was important to quilt the old-fashioned way, by hand. If you decide on hand quilting, choose fabrics that are soft and drape easily to give you the most ease of stitching. White tone-on-tone prints add more character and depth to a quilt than solids, but if you decide to use them, make sure that the printed designs are not too extensive. The surface of a tone-on-tone fabric should not feel rubbery to your fingertips. In fact, when you close your eyes and run your fingers over the fabric, you should not be able to feel any printing at all. Keep the same idea in mind when you select backing fabric.

When it comes to choosing the color for the "grout" (the sashing, border, and binding strips) for your quilt, look for one that will complement your main print(s) without being so dark that it overpowers the blocks.

You will be working closely with each of the fabrics in your quilt, so whatever your color choices, be sure to choose fabrics that you really love. A fabric you've decided on in haste (because the time on your parking meter ran out) may soon turn into one you do not enjoy working with. Quilts begun from these fabrics often end up in an unfinished-projects box.

Finally, whatever choices you make, start with favorite fabrics from your own stash so that you can use some of them up and make room for more!

SHOPPING TIPS

AS QUILTERS TODAY, we are lucky to have a great variety of fabrics to choose from. The following information will be helpful when you purchase fabrics for either a two-color or a scrap quilt.

- One fat quarter of fabric will yield nine 6" squares. One quarter yard will give you a minimum of six 6" squares. (Some fabrics are wider than others, so you may occasionally get seven squares from a quarter yard.)

- Check the cut edges of each fabric you consider buying. If it ravels too much, discard it. You will be turning under a very narrow edge of fabric as you appliqué, and fabric that frays tends to disappear as it ravels thread by thread.

- For a scrap quilt, you will need one 2¼-yard piece of a single foreground fabric and the same amount of a single main print in order to avoid having to piece the borders.

FABRIC PREPARATION

IT IS BEST to wash, dry, and iron all fabrics before you start any project. This will ensure the colorfastness of each fabric and prevent any later shrinkage when your finished quilt is laundered. I recommend using either Dreft or Woolite to wash white or light fabrics, using tepid water and a short washing cycle. Dry the fabrics in a hot dryer until they are completely dry. For darker fabrics, I use the same washing procedure, with Retayne rather than Dreft or Woolite. Dark fabrics, especially the indigo-dyed prints that I used, have a tendency to run, so it's a good idea to test them individually for colorfastness after they are dry. Cut a small piece from each fabric and immerse it in cool water. If any color seeps into the water, rewash and dry that fabric and test it again. If color continues to be released into the water, your best option may be to replace it with a different fabric.

BATTING

FOR HAND QUILTING, nothing beats the ease of stitching through 100%-polyester batting. It is soft and lightweight, and each stitch you take feels like you are quilting through butter. If you like the flat look of a vintage quilt, consider a low-loft polyester batting. If you like the look and feel of cotton batting, experiment with various lofts and brands to see what you like best.

For machine quilting, 100%-cotton battings, as well as cotton-polyester blends, are appropriate. Do not use 100%-polyester batting for machine quilting, because the fibers tend to be slippery, making it more difficult to manipulate a quilt through a sewing machine.

Recessed Appliqué

IN RECESSED APPLIQUÉ, a solid fabric or tone-on-tone print overlies a lower layer of print fabric. The quilter cuts out a shape in the top fabric to reveal the print underneath. The cutout shape includes a seam allowance inside the design area, which is then folded under and stitched down.

One of the things I like best about recessed appliqué is that it is so portable. There is no freezer paper to stiffen the fabric while you stitch, which makes it more pliable and soft. There is no need for soaking to remove the paper later on, either. Follow these steps for easy and effective recessed appliqué. The more blocks you stitch, the easier it will be to get into the rhythm of sweeping under the fabric edge and stitching down the fold.

1. Press a 6" square of foreground fabric so that it is flat and unwrinkled. Center a 4½" square acrylic ruler on the right side of the fabric and mark around it with a mechanical pencil. Place the marked square of fabric over the tile design of your choice from the "Tile Gallery" (pages 26–125). Align the corners of the marked square with the corners of the printed block, anchoring the fabric with painter's tape if necessary. Using the pencil, trace the design, including the single lines, onto the right side of the foreground fabric. If you wish, you can also mark lines to indicate shaded areas on your fabric,

as shown. A few pencil strokes will be enough to let you know at a glance which parts of the design are to be cut out.

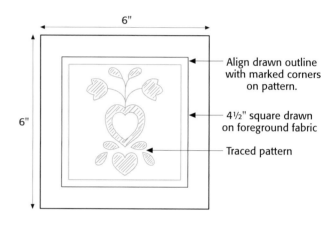

6"

6"

Align drawn outline with marked corners on pattern.

4½" square drawn on foreground fabric

Traced pattern

TIP

If your foreground fabric is dark, trace the design of your choice onto a piece of tracing paper, using a black permanent marking pen. Place the traced design on a light box and tape your marked 6" square of foreground fabric over it, aligning the corners. Using a light-colored, removable fabric-marking pen or pencil, trace the design onto the marked foreground square. It's a good idea to test any marking tool you wish to use on a scrap piece of the dark fabric to make sure that the marks are removable before you mark an actual quilt block.

RECESSED APPLIQUÉ AND REVERSE APPLIQUÉ

The word reverse *is defined in the dictionary as "opposite or contrary in position, direction, order, or character." In regard to quilting, the term* reverse appliqué *often makes people ask questions such as "Should I be sewing backward?" or "Should I be working from the back side of the fabric?" Because of this confusion, many people tend to shy away from reverse appliqué.*

The word recessed *is defined in the dictionary as "a receding part or space, an indentation in a line." Because this term is so much more descriptive of the process of stitching an upper layer of fabric to a lower layer, I prefer to use* recessed appliqué *rather than* reverse appliqué. *When my students realize how simple the process actually is, they are all, without fail, amazed at how hesitant they were to try it!*

I sincerely hope that the term reverse appliqué *will vanish completely from our quilting vocabulary and be replaced by the more accurate* recessed appliqué. *Using this new term may eliminate any intimidating or scary feelings quilters have about this enjoyable hand-stitching technique.*

2. Press a 6" main-print square. Pin the marked foreground square on top of the main-print square at the corners. Using a needle and thread, baste ¼" outside the marked lines of the design, as well as inside the corners of the 6" squares as shown. Baste as much as necessary to make sure that the two pieces of fabric will not shift while you appliqué. Remove the pins.

3. Starting inside a shaded area at the center of the block, cut away *only* the foreground fabric, leaving a ⅛" seam allowance.

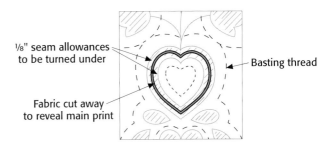

4. In order for the fabric to turn under without pulling, clip inside corners and curves. Clip sharp inner points, such as at the top of the heart, right up to the marked line. Also clip inside curves, keeping each clip just shy of the marked line.

Clip corners and curves.

5. Thread a needle with machine embroidery thread that matches the foreground fabric and knot the end of the thread. Bury the knot by bringing the needle up through the foreground fabric from the wrong side, exactly on the marked line at approximately the middle of the right side of the center heart. (If you are left-handed, bring the needle up at approximately the middle of the *left* side of the center heart.) Hold the block in your left hand, with your thumb close to the point where the thread comes up through the fabric. (If you are left-handed, hold the block in your right hand.) This is where you want to start turning under the fabric. With the needle in your right hand (if you are left-handed, hold the needle in your left hand), sweep the seam allowance under, so that the marked line is just out of sight.

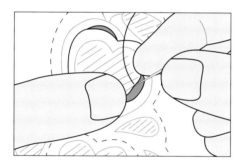

6. Holding the turned-under seam allowance securely with your left thumb, take one or two small stitches. (If you are left-handed, use your right thumb.) Stitch toward yourself, rather than from right to left. This technique allows you to see where you're going much more clearly than having to look over your thumb to see the fold. After every two or three stitches, give the thread a little tug to sink the thread down into the fabric. Just a light tug is all that's required; do not pull the fabric into puckers or pleats. Continue stitching in the same manner, sweeping the

TIP

Wherever two points meet, make sure that you leave one or two threads of the top fabric intact so that you will not create a gap between the stitched shapes. (See "Against the Flow" on page 28.)

fabric under, holding it securely, and taking one or two stitches at a time. Catch just a thread or two of the foreground fabric as you bring the needle up.

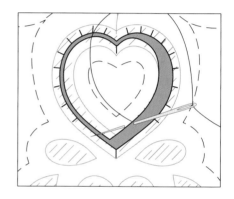

7. When you reach an outer point, such as the one at the bottom of the center heart, stitch right up to the marked line and take an extra stitch to anchor the point as shown. Then turn your fabric so that the sewing direction is toward you again and sweep the seam allowance under at the point. Give the thread a little tug to help make the point nice and sharp. Then begin stitching the other side of the heart.

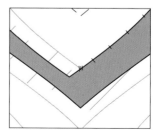

8. When you come to the inner point at the top of the heart, take a few extra stitches very close together as shown to prevent fraying.

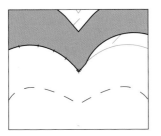

9. Stitch the remaining portion of the center heart design, bringing the needle all the way to the back side of your work after the final stitch. To end, take a few backstitches slightly to the inside of the heart, and clip the thread. Continue stitching the remaining portions of the design in the same manner, omitting the single lines. Press the completed block with a steam iron.

10. Stem stitch the single lines of the design, using two strands of embroidery floss in an embroidery needle. To do the stem stitch, bring your needle up at point A, move the needle to the right, and insert it into the fabric at point B. Bring the needle up again at point C, which is midway between A and B. Keep the thread below the needle at all times and keep A, B, and C about ⅛" apart. Insert the needle at point D. Bring the needle up again at point B. Continue stitching from left to right in the same manner. To end, bring the thread to the wrong side of the work. Take a few tiny backstitches on top of the stitched line and clip the thread.

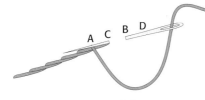

Stem Stitch

11. The Silver Bells block on page 99 also features French knots. To make a French knot, bring a knotted thread up at the point where you want to place the French knot. Wrap the thread around the needle twice. Holding the thread taut, insert the needle very close to the point where the thread comes out of the fabric. Bring the needle all the way to the wrong side of your work. Take one or two stitches near the beginning knot. Clip the thread, or simply bring the thread up again where you wish to place the next French knot.

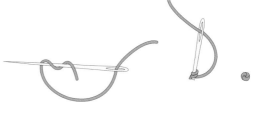

French Knot

12. Trim the finished appliqué block to 4½" square, using a rotary cutter, 4½" square acrylic ruler, and cutting mat. Do not use the marked lines as your cutting guides, as some distortion is inevitable in appliqué.

— TIP —

With a fine-tip permanent marking pen, mark diagonal lines on your 4½" square ruler. This will help you center the ruler on your finished block as you trim your blocks to size.

Deft Delft

WHETHER YOU CHOOSE to make all 196 designs or only a handful of your favorite blocks, your project will be unique. Every quilter has her own eye for block placement and her own preferences regarding fabric. Once you've made a quilt, use the following instructions as inspiration to try different settings, sashings, and fabrics. Or enlarge a single block to create a place mat or a framed picture for your next project.

MATERIALS

The fabric requirements listed here are based on fabric that measures at least 40" wide after washing.

Foreground fabric (or assorted scrap fabrics): 7¼ yards for blocks and borders

Main print (or assorted scrap fabrics): 7¼ yards for blocks and borders

Sashing and second border fabric: 2½ yards

Backing fabric: 5 yards

Binding fabric: ⅝ yard

Batting: 77" x 77" piece

CUTTING PLANS

IF YOU HAVE decided on only two fabrics for your quilt, use the information in the cutting list directly below. For a scrap quilt, refer to the cutting list on page 15.

Cutting for a Two-Fabric Quilt

Blocks are cut 6" square to allow for shrinkage and distortion during the appliqué process. After you have completed the appliqué, press and trim each block to 4½" square.

From the foreground fabric, cut lengthwise:
+ One 2¼-yard piece; from this piece, cut:
    4 strips, 5" x 80"
    4 strips, 1½" x 75"
    26 squares, 6" x 6"

From the remaining foreground fabric, cut:
+ 170 squares, 6" x 6"

From the main print, cut lengthwise:
+ One 2¼-yard piece; from this piece, cut:
    4 strips, 5" x 80"
    4 strips, 1½" x 75"
    26 squares, 6" x 6"

From the remaining main print, cut:
+ 170 squares, 6" x 6"

From the sashing and second border fabric, cut lengthwise:
- ✦ 4 strips, ¾" x 75"
- ✦ 2 strips, ¾" x 59¾"
- ✦ 15 strips, ¾" x 59¼"
- ✦ 182 strips, ¾" x 4½"

From the binding fabric, cut crosswise:
- ✦ 8 strips, 2¼" x 40"

Cutting for a Scrappy Quilt

Cut blocks 6" square to allow for shrinkage and distortion during the appliqué process. After you complete the appliqué, press and trim each block to 4½" square.

From one 2¼-yard piece of foreground fabric, cut lengthwise:
- ✦ 4 strips, 5" x 80"
- ✦ 4 strips, 1½" x 75"
- ✦ 26 squares, 6" x 6"

From assorted scrap foreground fabrics, cut:
- ✦ 170 squares, 6" x 6"

From one scrap main print, cut lengthwise:
- ✦ One 2¼-yard piece; from this piece, cut:
  4 strips, 5" x 80"
  4 strips, 1½" x 75"
  26 squares, 6" x 6"

From the assorted scrap main prints, cut:
- ✦ 170 squares, 6" x 6"

From the sashing and second border fabric, cut lengthwise:
- ✦ 4 strips, ¾" x 75"
- ✦ 2 strips, ¾" x 59¾"
- ✦ 15 strips, ¾" x 59¼"
- ✦ 182 strips, ¾" x 4½"

From the binding fabric, cut crosswise:
- ✦ 8 strips, 2¼" x 40"

PUTTING IT ALL TOGETHER

Before you mark and stitch the appliqué border, you will need to assemble the pieced section of the quilt top by sewing the 4½" blocks, the sashing strips, and the first and second borders together. This means that you can also admire your quilt top as you stitch your appliqué border!

Follow these steps to assemble the blocks and "grout"—the sashing strips.

1. Lay out the finished blocks in a grid of 14 x 14 in a place where you can see all of them together. This can be on a design wall or on the floor. Some of the blocks show more of the main print(s); these will catch the viewer's eye more quickly than the others. Arrange the more attention-getting blocks evenly throughout the quilt, so that the eye will travel evenly over the surface of the quilt.

2. Sew the blocks together in vertical rows, with ¾" x 4½" sashing strips between them. Press.

3. Sew the rows of blocks together with ¾" x 59¼" strips between them. Press. Add a ¾" x 59¼" strip to each side of the pieced section. Press. Add a ¾" x 59¾" strip to the top and the bottom of the pieced section. Press the completed section.

¾" x 59¾"

¾" x 59¼"

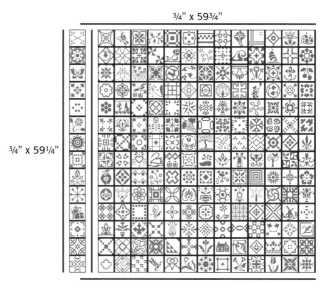

Adding the First and Second Borders

Follow these steps to sew the first and second border strips together before adding them to the quilt top.

1. For the first border, pin or thread baste a 1½" x 75" foreground strip on top of a 1½" x 75" main-print strip and treat them as one. Repeat for the remaining pairs of 1½" x 75" foreground and main-print strips.

2. Pin and stitch a ¾" x 75" second border strip to each of the basted first border strips. Press. The resulting pieced border strips should measure 1¾" x 75".

3. Pin the midpoint of each pieced border strip. Measure the quilt top from top to bottom (A) and side to side (B) through the middle.

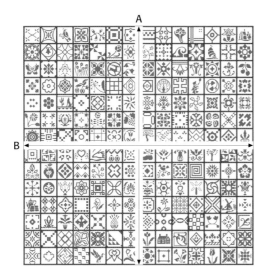

4. Divide the measurement of A by 2. Use pins to mark this measurement on either side of the midpoint on two of the pieced border strips. These pins correspond to the corners of the quilt top. Sew these two pieced border strips to the sides of the quilt top, starting and ending ¼" in from the corners.

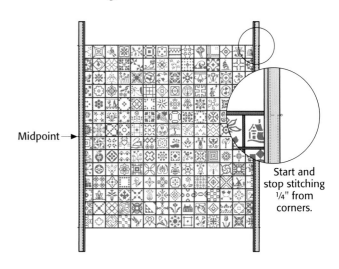

Midpoint →

Start and stop stitching ¼" from corners.

5. Using measurement B from step 3, repeat step 4 to attach the remaining pieced border strips to the top and bottom of the quilt top.

6. Place one corner of the quilt on the ironing board with the side border on top of the top border, as shown.

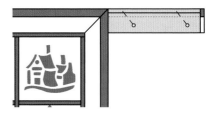

7. Fold the side border strip under at a 45° angle, so that it lies exactly on top of the top border. Pin these borders right sides together, as shown. Press the angled fold.

8. Fold the quilt top up to reveal the pressed fold line. This will be the stitching line for the mitered corner seam. Pin the two border strips together across the fold line. Stitch the corner seam exactly along the fold line.

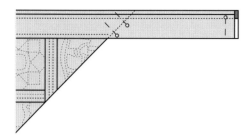

9. Trim the seam allowance to ¼". Open up the seam allowance and press.

10. Repeat steps 6 through 9 to miter the remaining three border corner seams.

ADDING THE APPLIQUÉ BORDER

To CUSTOM-FIT the appliqué border strips to your quilt top, you will need to prepare one tracing-paper border for the sides of your quilt and a second tracing-paper border for the top and bottom edges.

Preparing the Tracing-Paper Borders

1. Measure your quilt top from top to bottom and from side to side through the middle to find measurements A and B, referring to "Adding the First and Second Borders" on page 16.

2. Unroll an 80" length of tracing paper and tape it down on a flat surface. Using a black permanent marking pen, draw a border that is 4" wide by measurement A of your quilt top, which should be approximately 62¼" long. This is the finished size of the side appliqué borders. Mark the midpoint and half the distance of A on either side of the midpoint.

3. Tape the midpoint of the tracing-paper border on top of the border motif on page 125. Trace the border motif onto the center of the tracing-paper border. Trace the border motif seven times on either side of the center motif. This tracing-paper border will be for the sides of the quilt.

4. Referring to step 2, mark a second tracing-paper border that measures 4" by measurement B of your quilt top, which should be approximately 70¼" long. This is the finished size of the top and bottom appliqué borders. Mark the midpoint of this border, and mark half the distance of B on either side of the midpoint. Trace the border motif from page 125 onto the center of the tracing-paper border. Trace the border motif seven times on either side of the center motif, leaving the corner areas unmarked. This tracing-paper border will be for the top and bottom of the quilt.

5. Tape the two tracing-paper borders together at a right angle, forming a corner as shown. Trace the corner design from page 125 onto both ends of the longer tracing-paper border. If your A and B measurements were slightly different, you may need to adjust the corner lines, referring to the diagram.

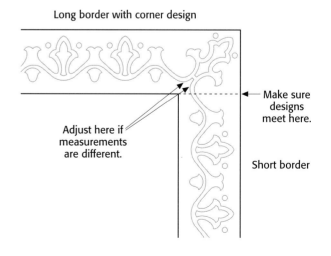

Long border with corner design

Make sure designs meet here.

Adjust here if measurements are different.

Short border

Stitching the Appliqué Border Strips

1. Fold a 5" x 80" foreground strip in half to find the midpoint. Thread baste across the midpoint of this strip. Measure half the distance of A on either side of the midpoint and baste across the strip at these points. Also baste a seam line ½" in from one long edge of the foreground strip. Repeat for one 5" x 80" foreground strip.

5. Baste each 5" x 80" foreground strip on top of a 5" x 80" main-print strip and treat them as one. Appliqué the border strips, referring to "Recessed Appliqué" on page 10. Press the completed border strips. Trim the bottom edge to ¼" from the basted seam line on each foreground strip. You will trim the other edge of these border strips when you add the binding.

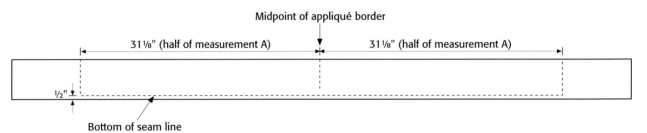

Midpoint of appliqué border

31⅛" (half of measurement A)   31⅛" (half of measurement A)

½"

Bottom of seam line

2. Pin a basted 5" x 80" foreground strip on top of the shorter tracing-paper border, matching the centers and bottom seam lines. Using a pencil, trace 15 border motifs onto the fabric. Repeat with a second 5" x 80" foreground strip. Do *not* trim these border strips to a shorter length.

3. Repeat steps 1 and 2, using measurement B of your quilt top to baste two 5" x 80" foreground strips. Measure 4" from the basted lines at the ends of each strip to find the corner point. Baste across the strips at the corner points.

4. Pin a basted 5" x 80" foreground strip on top of the longer tracing-paper border, matching the centers, corner points, and bottom seam lines. Using a pencil, trace 15 border motifs onto the fabric. Also trace the corner designs, adjusting the lines if necessary. Remove the tracing paper. Repeat with the remaining 5" x 80" foreground strip.

6. Sew the two appliqué border strips without corner motifs to the sides of the quilt top. Press and trim the side borders even with the top and bottom edges of the quilt top.

7. Sew the two appliqué border strips with the corner motifs to the top and bottom of the quilt top, being careful to match the corner motifs to the side border motifs. Press. Trim the top and bottom borders even with the edges of the quilt top.

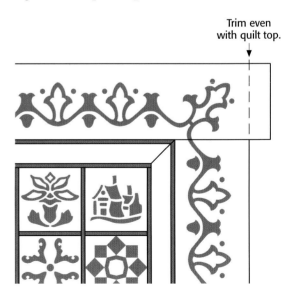

Trim even with quilt top.

8. Press the completed quilt top.

FINISHING

AFTER YOU DECIDE whether you wish to quilt by hand or machine, and after you choose the batting you want to use, follow the next steps to prepare the quilt sandwich for quilting.

Preparing the Quilt Sandwich

Unfold the batting the day before you plan to use it, so that the fibers will relax, and follow these steps to prepare the backing and layer the quilt sandwich:

1. Cut the backing fabric in half along the crosswise grain. Cut one of these pieces along the lengthwise grain to create two narrow pieces equal in width. Sew the two narrow pieces to the sides of the uncut length of backing fabric. Press the seam allowances open. Trim to 77" x 77" square.

Half width	Full width	Half width

2. Tape the pressed backing wrong side up on a table or clean floor. Make sure that it is taut but not stretched.

3. Place the batting on top of the backing, smoothing out any creases and wrinkles as you go.

4. Place the quilt top right side up on top of the batting. Thread baste the three layers together, starting at the center of the quilt sandwich and working out toward the edges. Because the blocks are 4" square, it is easy to use the "grout" or sashing strips as the basting areas. This has the advantage of keeping the blocks free of the basting thread while you quilt.

Starting in the middle of the quilt,
thread baste through sashing.

5. Finally, fold the raw edges of the backing over to the right side of the quilt sandwich and baste them in place to prevent the raw edges from raveling while you quilt.

Quilting

It isn't a quilt unless it's quilted! I outline quilted ⅛" around all parts of the designs and around the sashing strips as well. In the second border, I used the continuous-line cable design shown in actual size here. You can use the same quilting approaches I did, or choose designs that appeal to you.

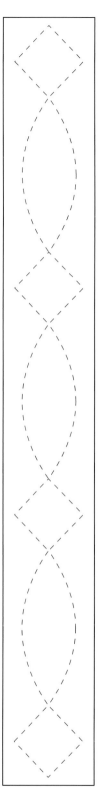

Continuous Quilting Design for First Border
Adjust as necessary.

Binding

The instructions that follow are for double-fold French binding. If you wish to use a different method, you may need to alter the width of your binding strips.

1. After you finish quilting, use a rotary cutter, mat, and ruler to trim the edges of the quilt even. The borders should measure 4¼" wide.

2. Stitch the binding strips together end to end, using diagonal seams. Trim the seam allowances to ¼". Press the seams open. Fold the binding in half lengthwise with wrong sides together and press. Insert a walking foot in your sewing machine. Leave about a 6" tail of binding free. Then, starting at the middle on one side of the quilt and aligning the edge of the binding with the edge of the quilt, sew the binding to the quilt.

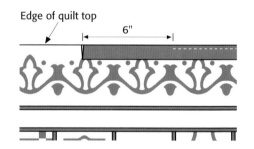

3. When you come to a corner, stop ¼" from the edge. Lift the presser foot and pivot to bring the next side of the quilt sandwich around. Raise the needle out of the fabric and pull the quilt toward you just enough to clear the presser foot. Lift the binding at a 45° angle and then bring it back down on itself, creating a fold at the corner.

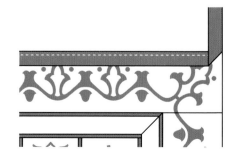

4. Using a ¼"-wide seam allowance, stitch through the fold and down the next side of the quilt sandwich. Repeat to miter the remaining three corner seams.

5. Continue stitching the final portion of the binding, stopping approximately 5" from where you started. Cut the threads. Open the binding strips and fold them perpendicular to each other, as shown. Press the angled folds carefully.

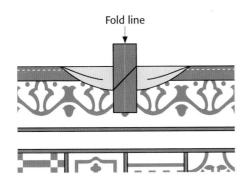

Fold line

6. Stitch the binding strips together along the pressed fold lines. Trim the seam allowance to ¼" and finger-press the seam open. Fold the binding wrong sides together and stitch the final portion of the binding to the quilt sandwich.

7. Fold the binding over the raw edges to the back of the quilt. Slip-stitch the binding in place, so that it just covers your machine stitches. Form a miter at each corner and slip-stitch it closed on both the front and the back side of the quilt.

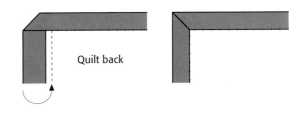

Quilt back

Labeling Your Quilt

It is important for your quilt to have a label! Using a permanent marking pen and a small square or rectangle of light fabric, inscribe the name of the quilt, your name as the quiltmaker, and the date you finished the quilt. You can add whatever else you feel is important. If you have access to a computer, consider one of its many fonts to design your label. Print out the information you desire and trace it onto your fabric with the permanent marking pen. Heat-set the ink with a hot, dry iron and appliqué the label to the lower right corner of the quilt backing.

Parisian Nine Patch

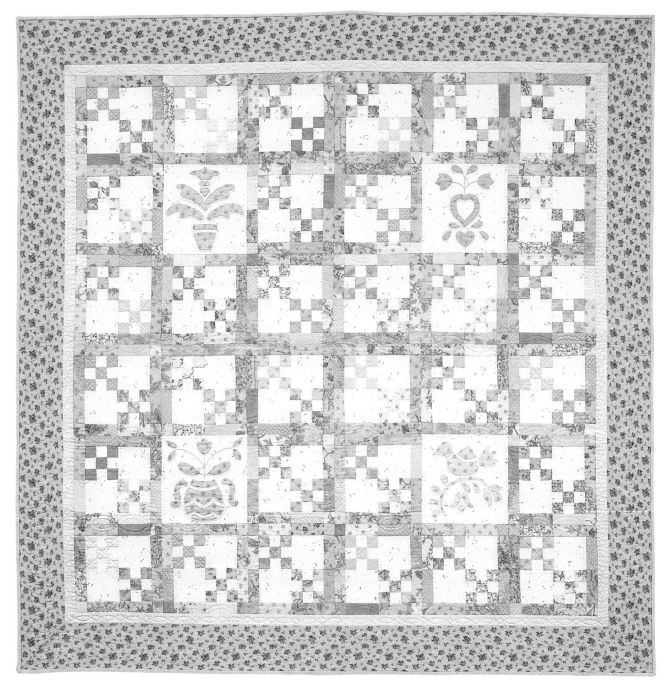

By Judy Garden, Connecticut, 61" x 61", 2003.

This quilt features the pieced Victory block and four appliqué blocks, including "Love Grows" (page 75),
"Sunny Day" (page 110), "African Violet" (page 28), and "Songbird" (page 101). I enlarged these designs 200%
to a finished size of 8". I used 36 different fabrics as main prints in this quilt, and their soft coloring
gives it a completely different look from the "Deft Delft" quilt shown on page 4.

MATERIALS

The fabric requirements are based on fabric that measures at least 40" wide after washing.

Main print: 36 *different* fat eighths for pieced blocks

Foreground fabric : 2 yards for pieced and appliqué blocks

First border fabric: ½ yard

Second border fabric: 1½ yards

Backing: 4 yards

Binding: ½ yard

Batting: 62" x 62" piece

Embroidery floss: 4 skeins of embroidery floss to match main prints in appliqué blocks

CUTTING

THE APPLIQUÉ BLOCKS are cut 10" square to allow for shrinkage and distortion during the appliqué process. After the appliqué is completed, press and trim each block to 8½" square.

From *each* of 4 main-print fat eighths, cut:
*   1 square, 10" x 10"

From *each* of the 32 remaining main-print fat eighths, cut:
*   3 strips, 1½" x 10"
*   8 rectangles, 1½" x 3½"
*   4 squares, 1½" x 1½"

From the foreground fabric, cut:
*   4 squares, 10" x 10"
*   96 strips, 1½" x 10"
*   64 squares, 3½" x 3½"'

From the first border fabric, cut:
*   8 strips, 1½" x 40"

From the second border fabric, cut:
*   8 strips, 6" x 40"

From the backing fabric:
*   Cut the fabric in half crosswise to make 2 pieces, 40" x 62"

From the binding fabric, cut:
*   7 strips, 2¼" x 40"

STITCHING THE APPLIQUÉ BLOCKS

FOR THE FOLLOWING steps, refer to "Recessed Appliqué" on page 10.

1. Using a photocopy machine, enlarge the patterns for "Love Grows" (page 75), "Sunny Day" (page 110), "African Violet" (page 28), and "Songbird" (page 101) by 200%.

2. Using an acrylic ruler and a mechanical pencil, mark an 8½" square on the right side of one of the 10" foreground squares. Place the marked square on top of one of the four appliqué designs, aligning the corners. Trace the appliqué design onto the foreground square and mark a few lines inside each shaded area.

3. Place the marked foreground square on top of one of the 10" main-print squares. Make sure that the wrong side of the foreground fabric lies on top of the right side of the main-print square. Pin the squares together at the corners and thread baste around each portion of the appliqué design.

4. Starting at the center of the block, cut the foreground fabric in a shaded area and appliqué that portion of the design. Repeat to stitch all remaining portions of the design. Press the block with a steam iron.

5. If there are single lines in the design, embroider them in stem stitch, using two strands of embroidery floss. Press the completed block.

—————— TIP ——————

I like to start with the appliqué blocks and hang them on my design wall by my sewing machine when they are finished, so that I can look at them while I piece the Victory blocks.

6. Repeat steps 2 through 5 for the remaining three appliqué blocks and trim all the blocks to 8½" x 8½", using an acrylic ruler and rotary cutter. Do not use the marked lines on the foreground fabric as your cutting lines, because some distortion is inevitable in appliqué.

PIECING THE VICTORY BLOCKS

EACH OF THE 32 pieced blocks in this quilt contains two nine-patch units. Each nine-patch unit is made from main-print strips and foreground strips.

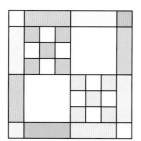

1. For strip set A, sew together two 1½" x 10" foreground strips and one 1½" x 10" main-print strip. For strip set B, sew together two 1½" x 10" main-print strips and one 1½" x 10" foreground strip. Press the seam allowances toward the main-print fabric. These strip sets should measure 3½" x 10".

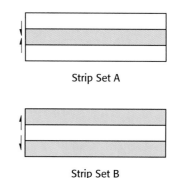

Strip Set A

Strip Set B

2. From strip set A, cut two 1½"-wide segments. From strip set B, cut four 1½"-wide segments. Sew two B segments to either side of an A segment. Repeat to make a second nine-patch unit. Press the seam allowances toward the main-print fabric. The two nine-patch units should measure 3½" x 3½".

3. Repeat steps 1 and 2 to make the remaining 62 nine-patch units, half with a strip set A segment in the middle and half with a strip set B segment in the middle. From each different main print, you will get two identical nine-patch units. Make sure that all of your nine-patch units measure 3½" x 3½".

4. Sew together eight 1½" x 3½" main-print rectangles, four 1½" x 1½" main-print squares, two 3½" x 3½" foreground squares, and two nine-patch units, as shown on page 25.

5. Press. Make sure that the completed block measures 8½" x 8½", trimming the edges slightly, if necessary. Make a total of 32 Victory blocks.

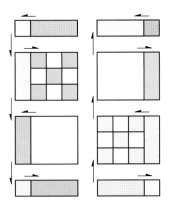

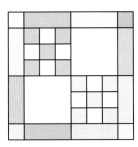

6. Arrange eight Victory blocks and one appliqué block, as shown, to create a quarter section of the quilt. Sew the blocks together in rows, and press. Sew the rows together to complete the quarter section. Press. Make three more quarter sections, using the remaining Victory and appliqué blocks.

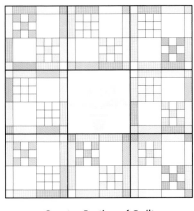

Quarter Section of Quilt

7. Sew the quarter sections together, and press.

ADDING THE BORDERS

FOLLOW THESE STEPS to add the first and second borders.

1. Sew together the eight 1½" x 40" first border strips end to end in sets of two. Repeat for the eight 6" x 40" second border strips.

2. Sew a 1½" x 80" first border strip lengthwise to each of the four 6" x 80" second border strips. These four pieced borders should measure approximately 7¼" x 80".

3. Sew the four pieced borders to the quilt top, referring to "Adding the First and Second Borders" on page 16. Press the completed quilt top.

FINISHING

FOLLOW THESE STEPS to prepare the quilt sandwich, quilt, and bind the quilt.

1. Layer and baste the quilt sandwich, referring to "Preparing the Quilt Sandwich" on page 25.

2. Quilt by hand or machine, referring to "Quilting" on page 20.

3. Bind the quilt, referring to "Binding" on page 20 and add a label to the backing, referring to "Labeling Your Quilt" on page 21.

Tile Gallery

Ｔ HERE ARE 196 tile designs in this gallery. You can make your own "Deft Delft" quilt, using all of them, or make a smaller project, like the one shown below, with the ones you like best.

PADDINGTON STATION *by Judy Garden, Connecticut, 48" x 48", 2003.*

*This quilt features two of the tile blocks in the "Tile Gallery": "Square Dance" (page 108)
and "Chocolate Box" (page 42). I enlarged these designs 200% to create 8" finished blocks, and
I designed and added a third block as a filler between the corner blocks.*

5 of Diamonds

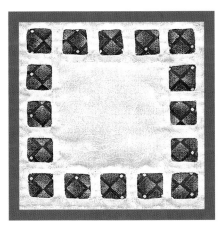

90 Degrees

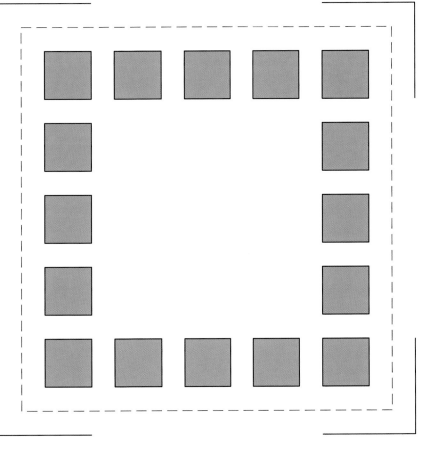

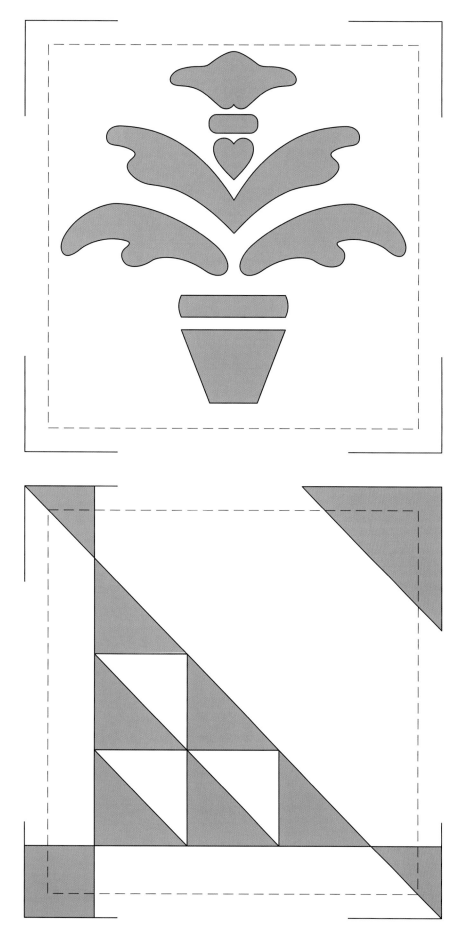

African Violet

Against the Flow

Almonds

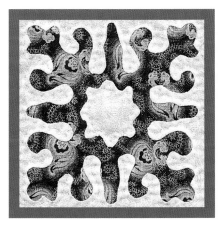

Amoeba

Apple Core

Awaken

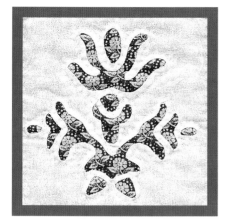

Aztec

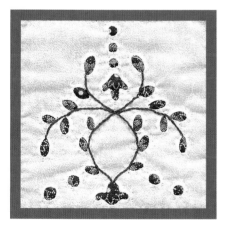

Baby's Breath

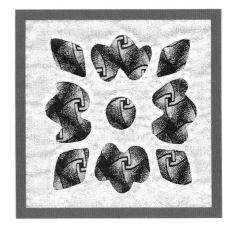

Bean Bags

Blue Bells

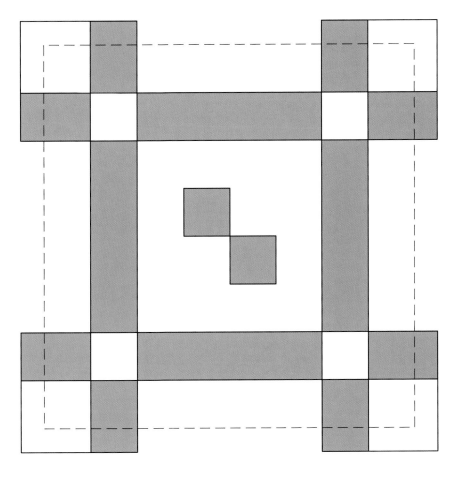

Border Crossings

Brooch

Brunch

Building Blocks

Bunnies

Busting Out

Butterfly

Cairncroft

Camera

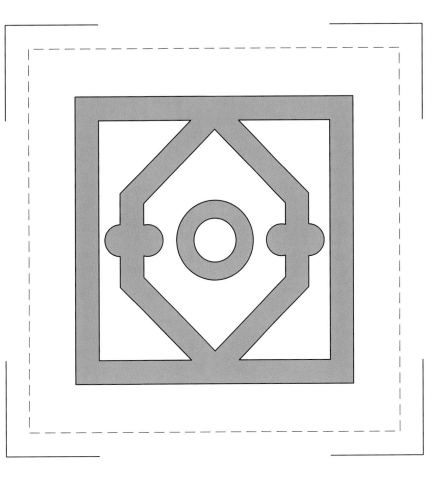

Canada Goose

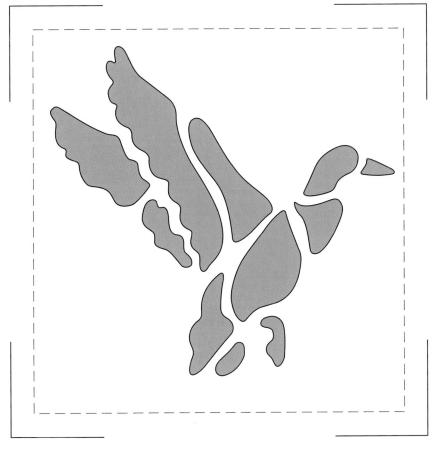

Capstone

Card Game

Carousel

Castle Window

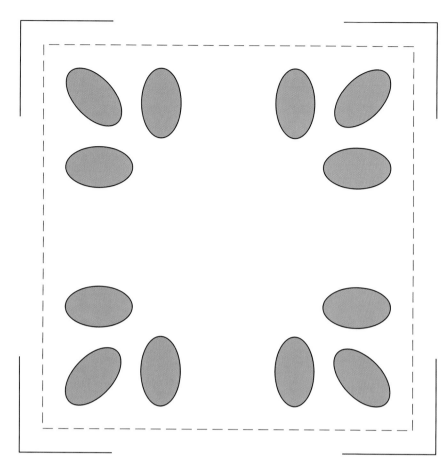

Cat's Paw

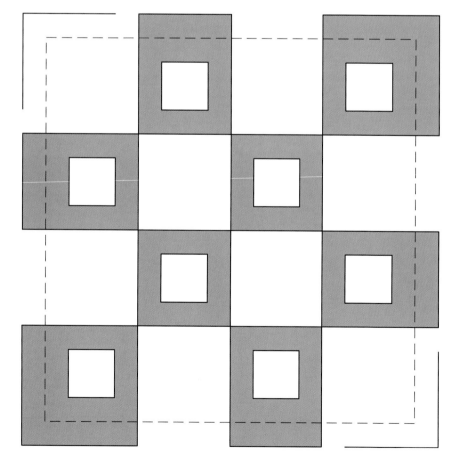

Checkers

Cherries

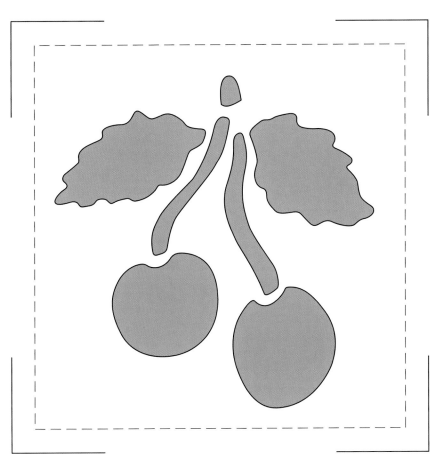

Chiclets

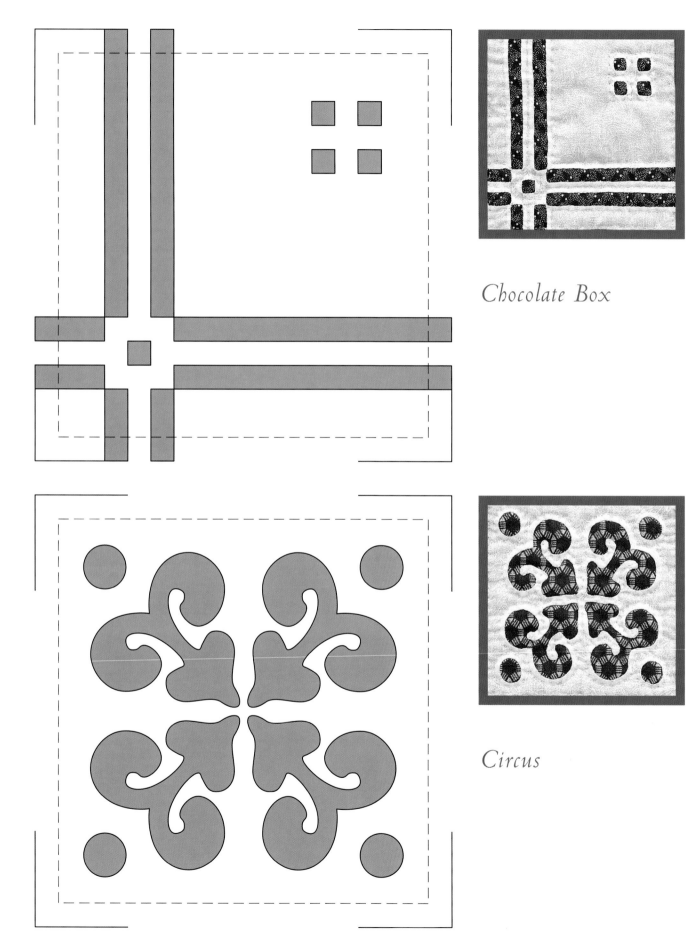

Chocolate Box

Circus

Clasp

Clowns

Coat of Arms

Cocoon

Conception

Cookie

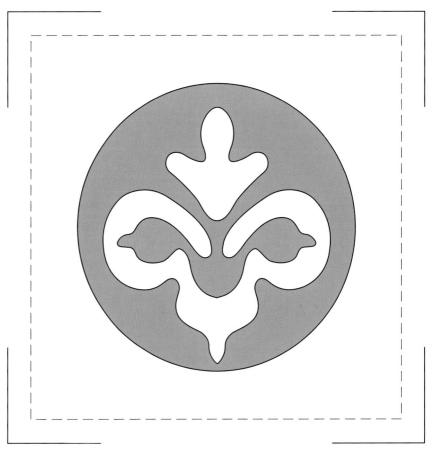

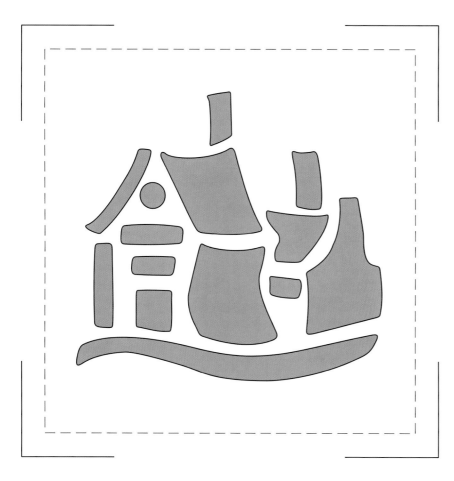

Cottage

Court Jester

Courtyard

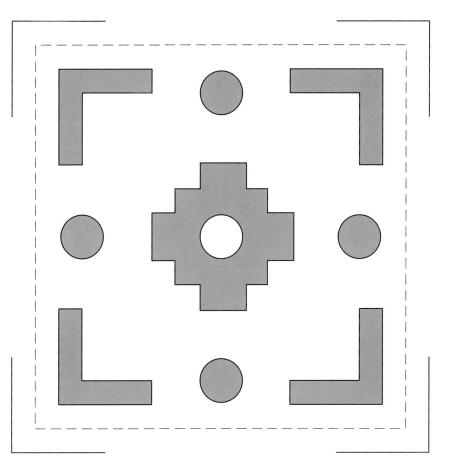

Coyote

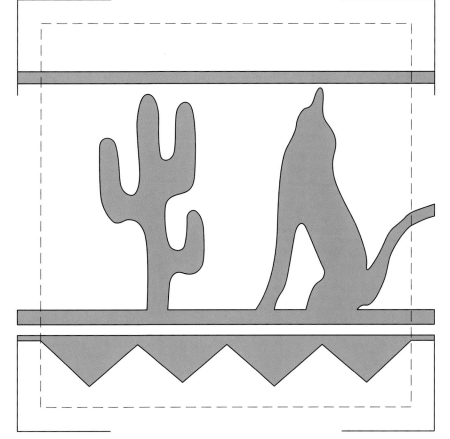

Crest

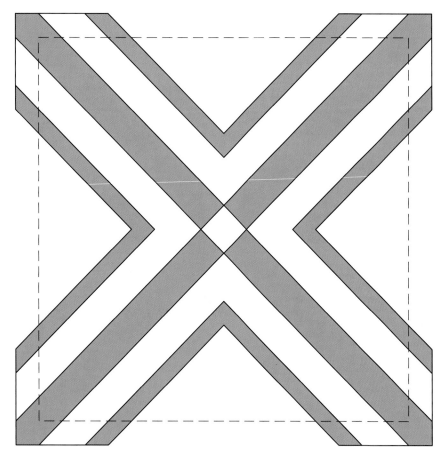

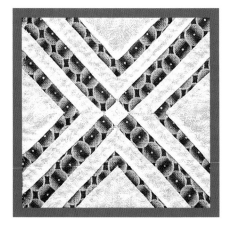

Crossroads

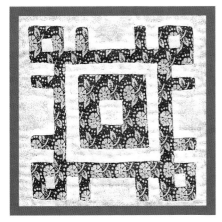

Crossword

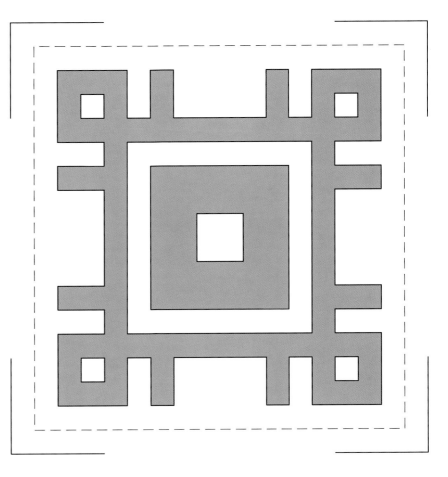

Crown Molding

Daisy

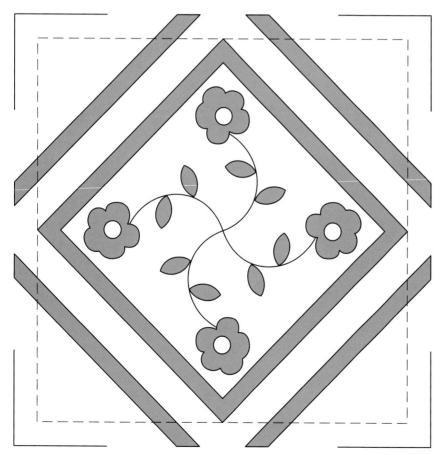

Dancing Daisies

Dandelion

Dauphin

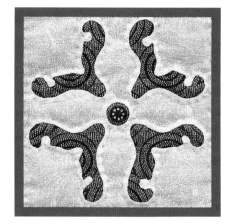

Deer

Diadem

Diamond Square

Dinner Party

Doily

Dolphins

Door Bell

Earrings

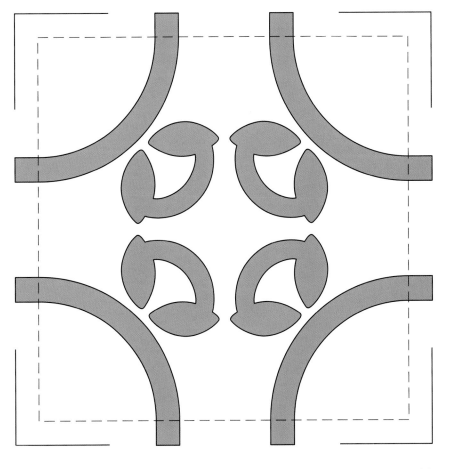

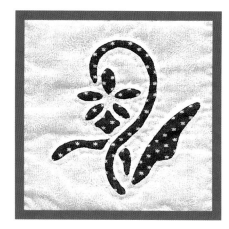

Edelweiss

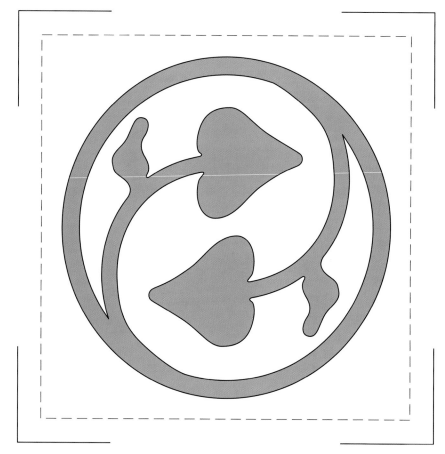

Entwined

Epaulet

Evening Star

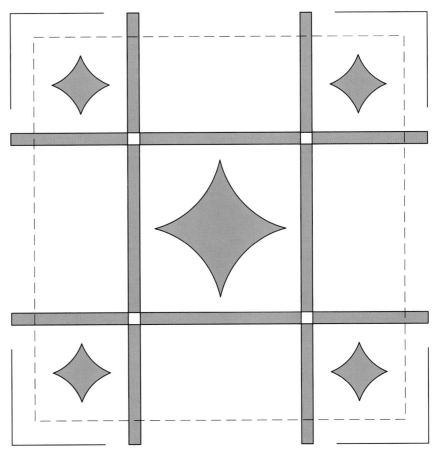

Family Tree

Fan

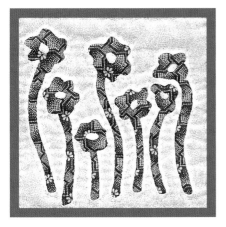

Field of Dreams

First Date

Flower Basket

Flower Pot

Flower Tag

French Urn

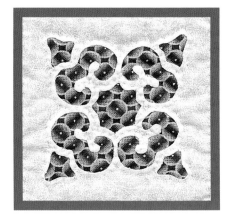

Frets

Funny Face

Gaia

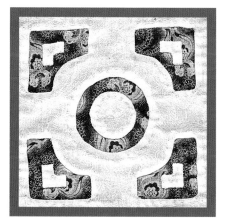

Garden

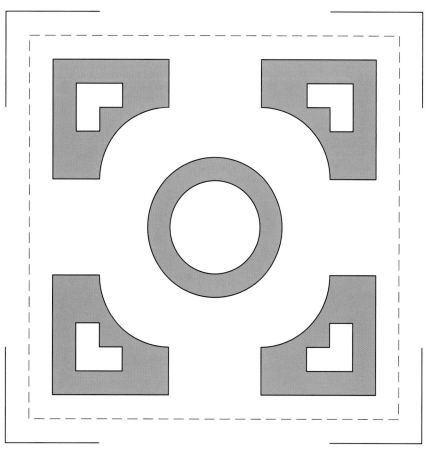

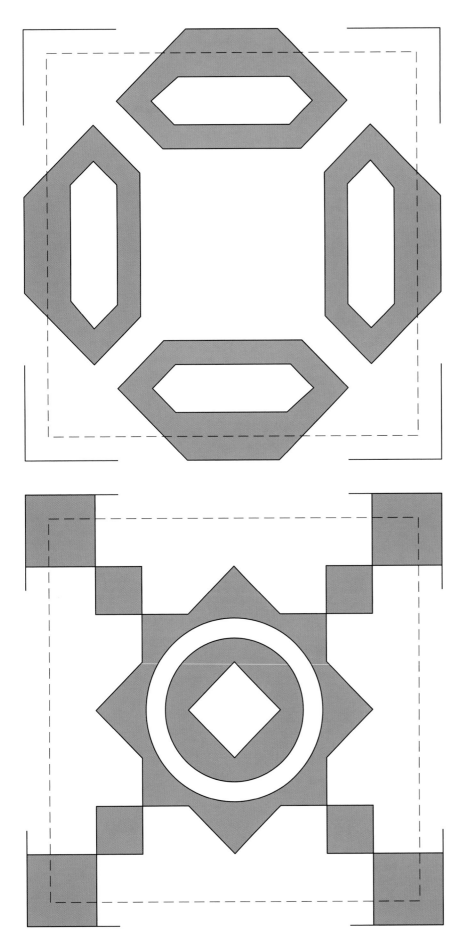

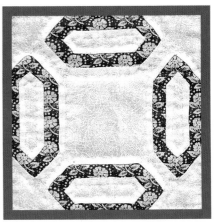

Gems

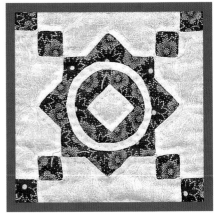

Geometry in Motion

Goldfish

Greeting Card

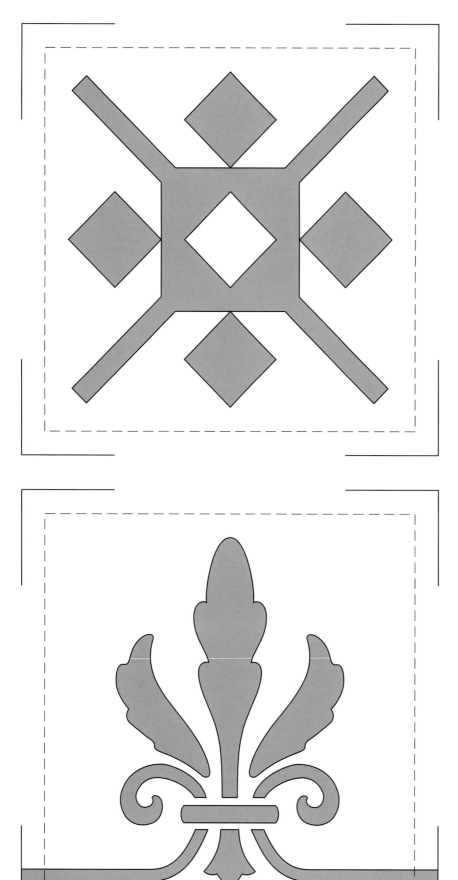

Harlequin

Head Dress

Heart

Highway

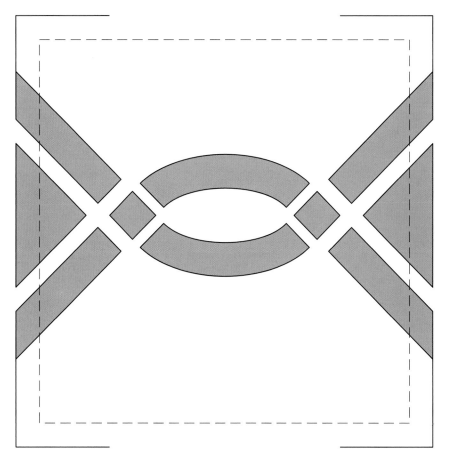

Hurricane

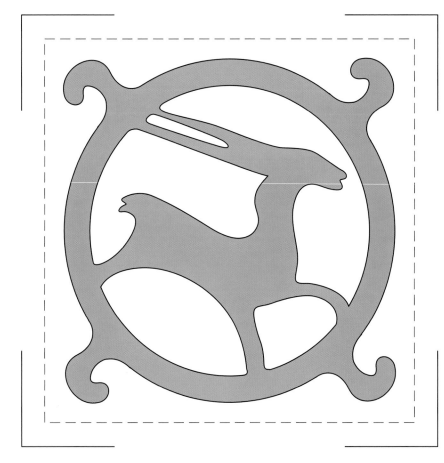

Impala

Inlay

Iris

Ivy League

Jigsaw

Kaleidoscope

King Arthur

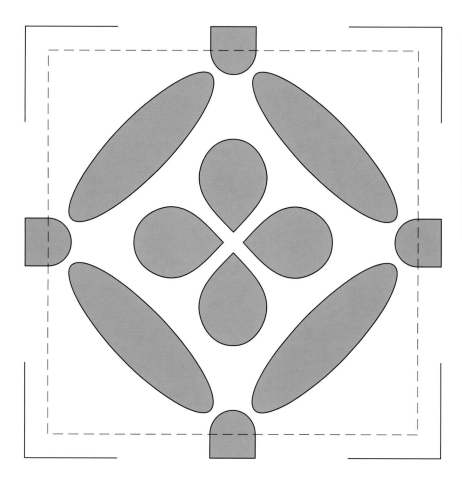

Kiwi

Lace

Lattice

Lily

Lizard

Logo

Lotus

Love Grows

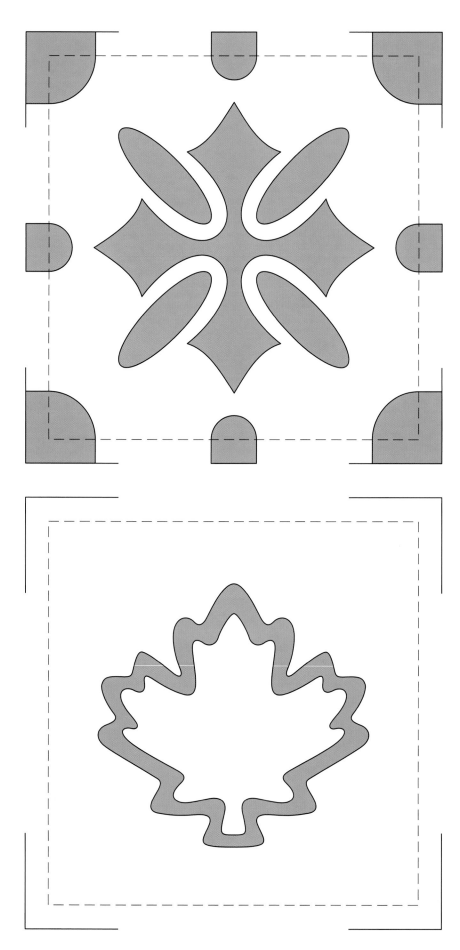

Maltese Cross

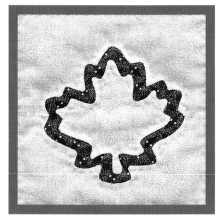

Maple Leaf

Marina

Marks the Spot

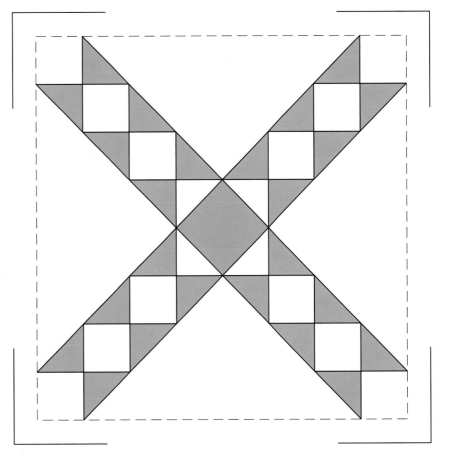

Mata Hari

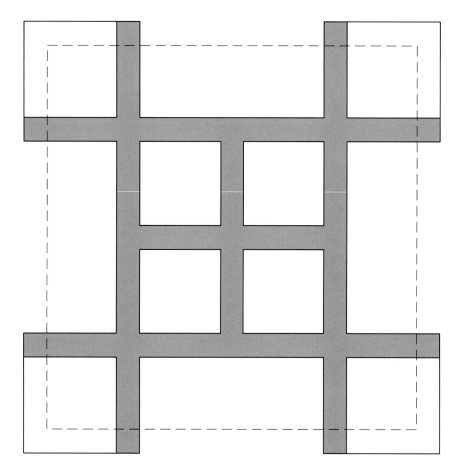

Matrix

Maze

Mums

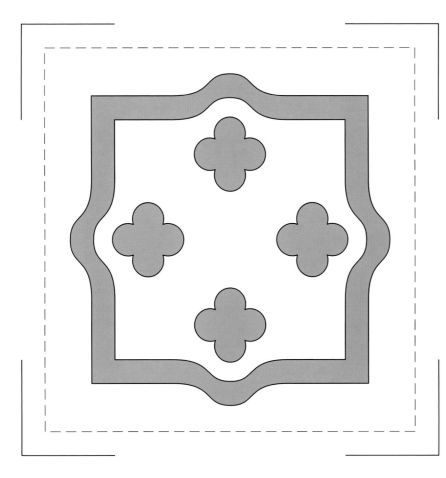

Musketeer

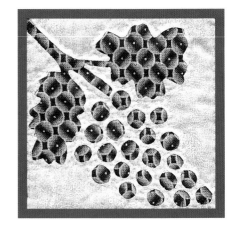

Napa Valley

Nesting

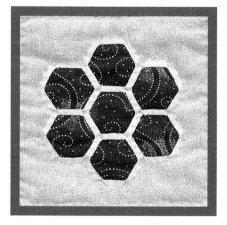

Neutral Zone

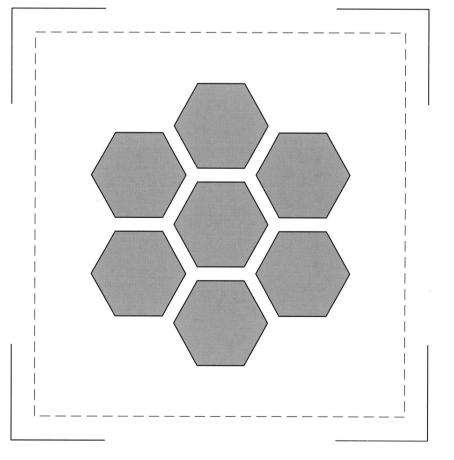

Night Light

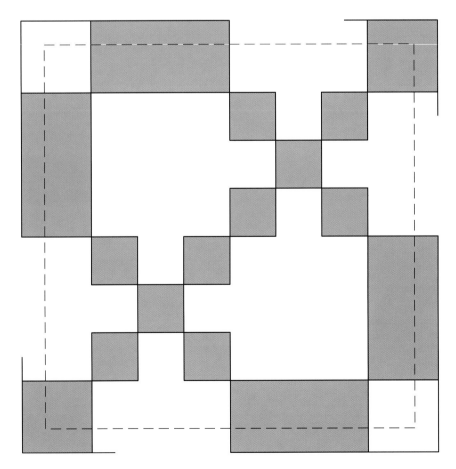

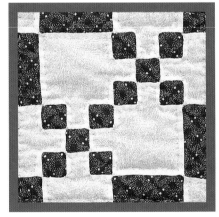

Nine Patch

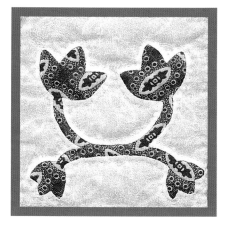

Old and New

Oranges and Lemons

Orbits

Order

Paper Planes

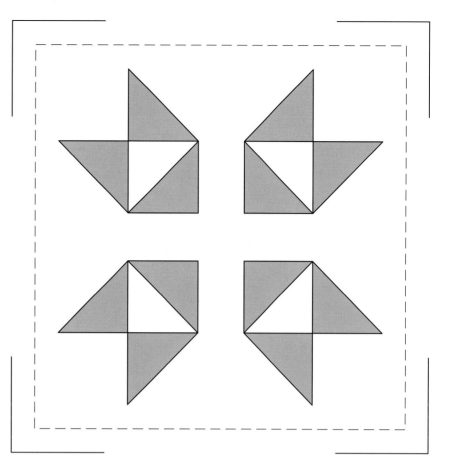

Parsley

Partridge

Pea Pod

Phazer

Piazza

Picture Frames

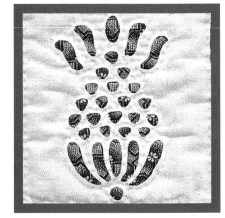

Pineapple

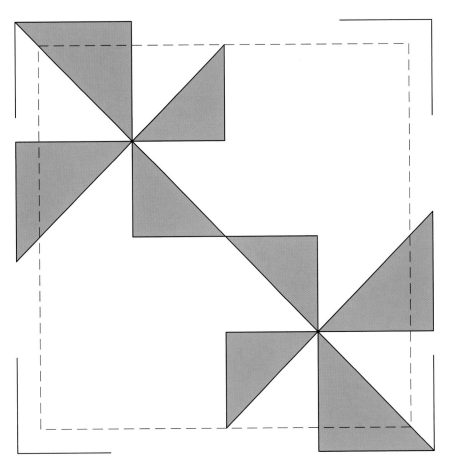

Pinwheel

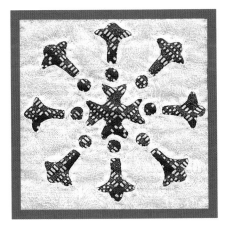

Plantaganet

Poirot

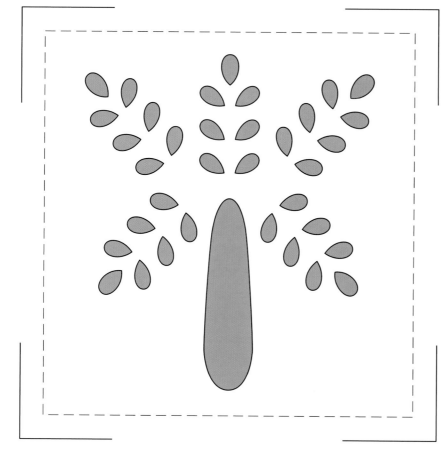

Pussy Willow

Pyramid

Queen of Spades

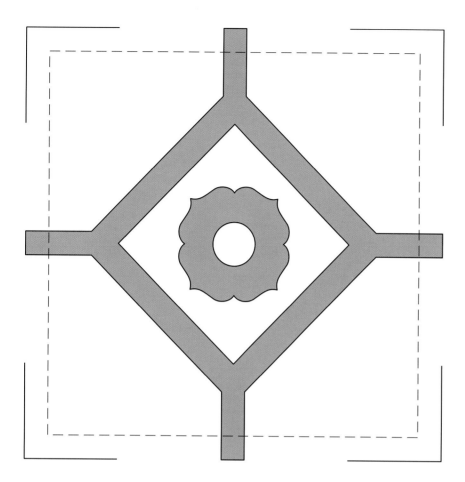

Remembrance

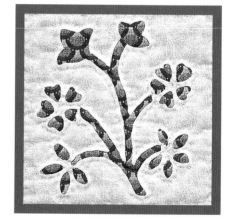

Riot of Growth

Rotunda

Sailboat

Salt and Pepper

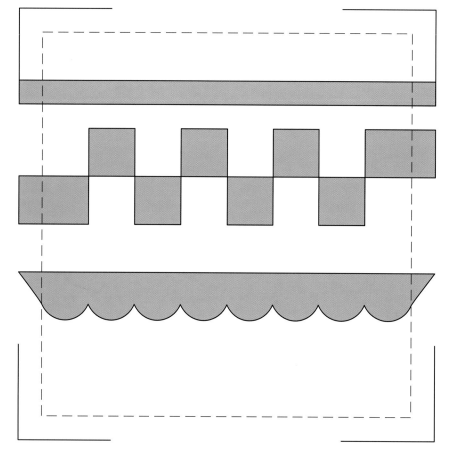

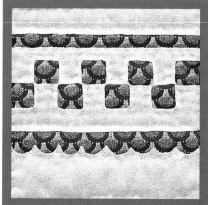

Scallop

School House

Sconce

Sea Wave

Searching

Segments

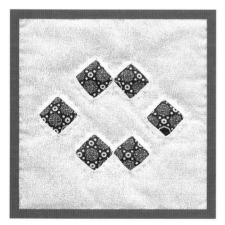

Separate Tables

Shapes

Shasta Daisy

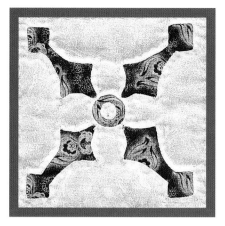

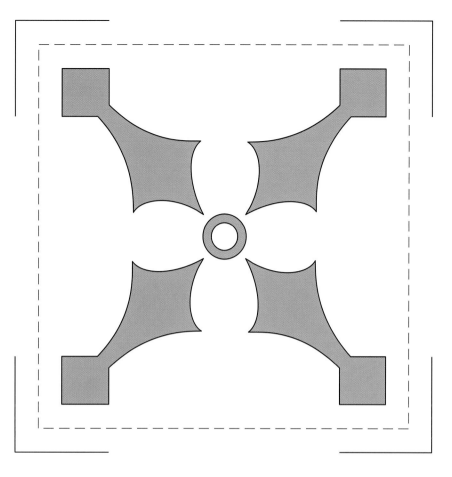

Shooting Stars

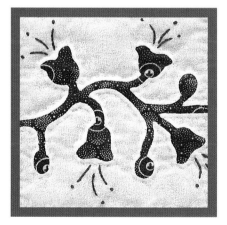

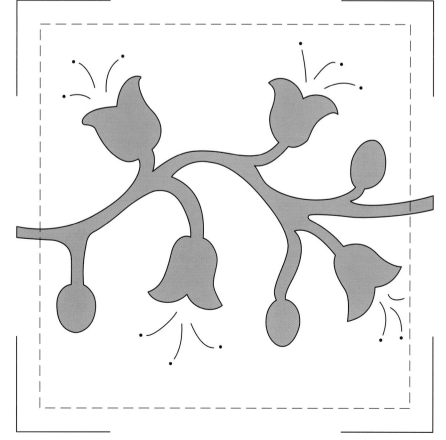

Silver Bells

Singleton

Smarties

Snowflake

Songbird

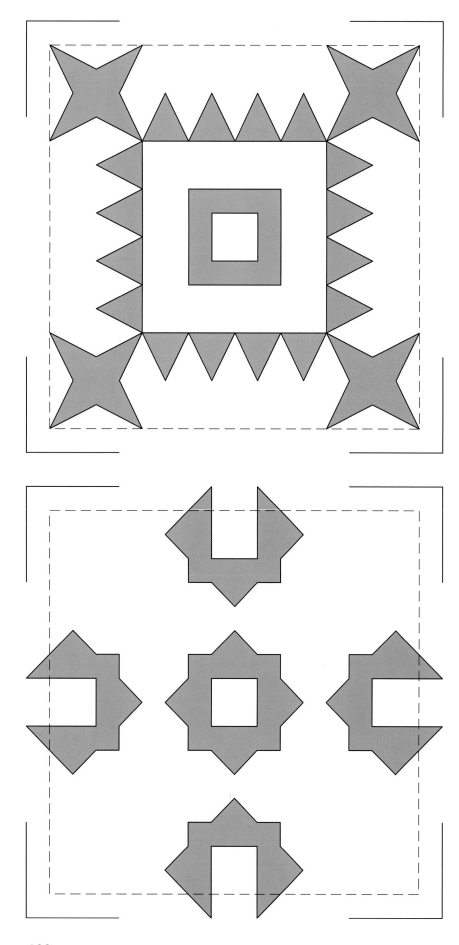

Southwest

Space Invaders

Spacemen

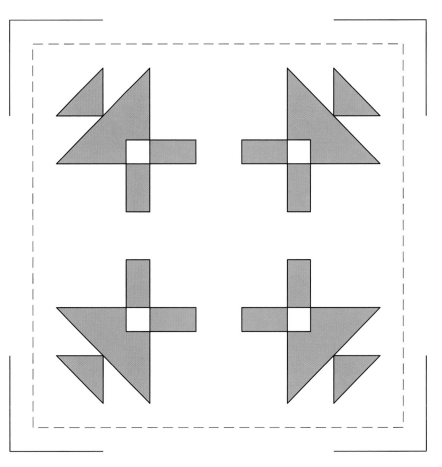

Spears

Spinning Star

Spinning Wheel

Spirograph

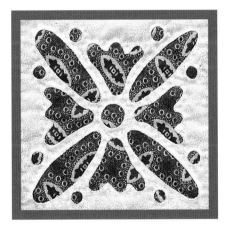

Splash

Sprig

Spring Growth

Sprites

Sprout

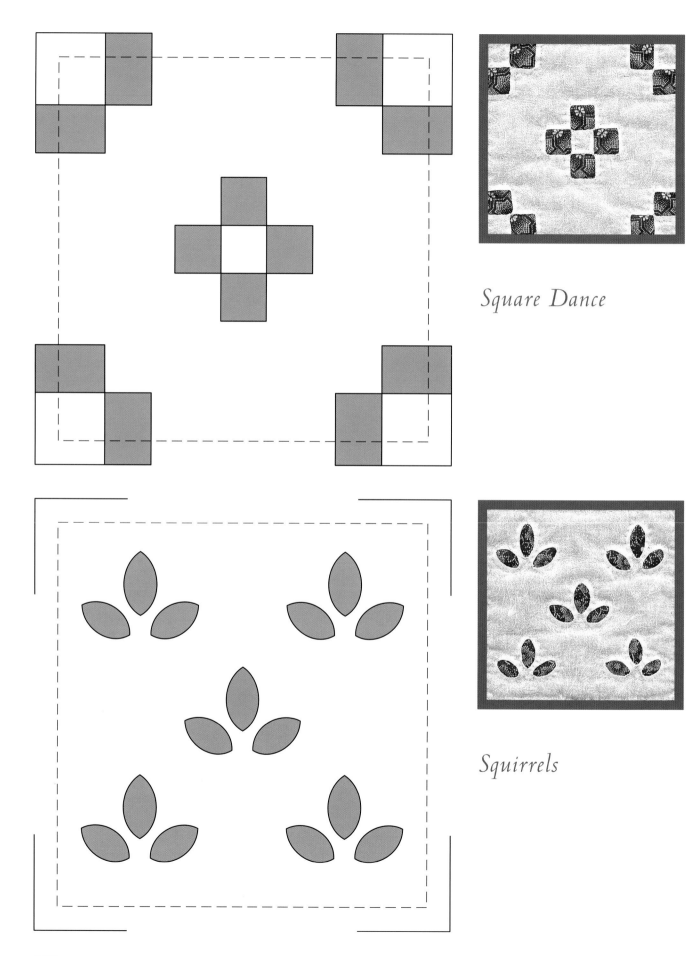

Square Dance

Squirrels

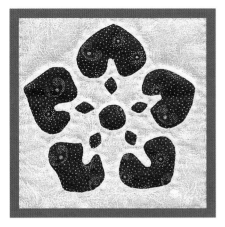

Star Fruit

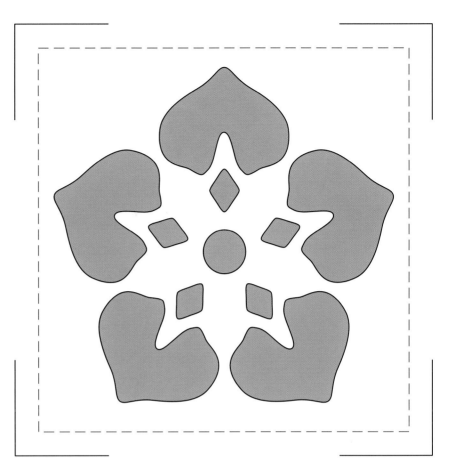

Steps

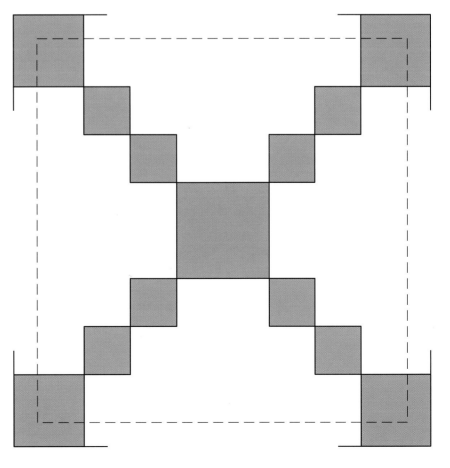

Sun Burst

Sunny Day

Swan

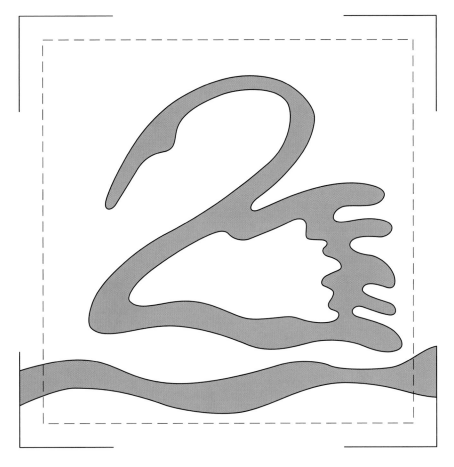

Sweet Pea

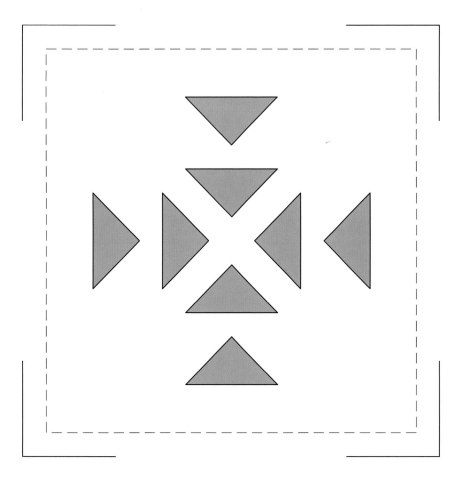

Target

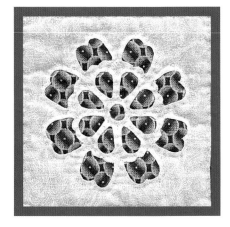

Tea Cakes

Teddy

Test Pattern

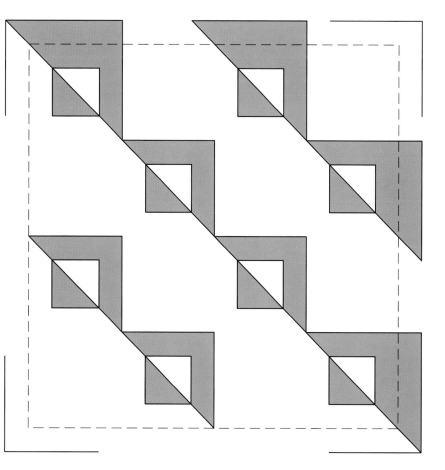

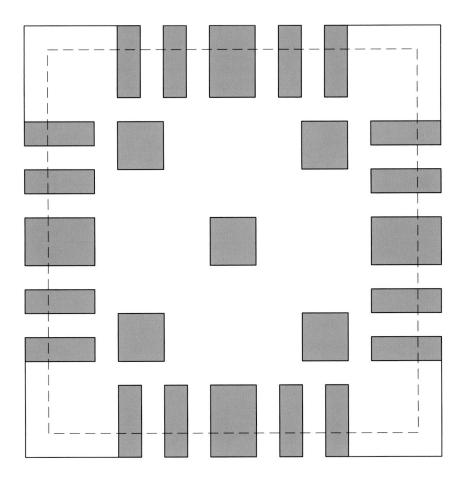

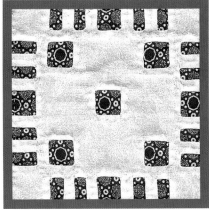

Tetrus

The Alps

Tiara

Time Warp

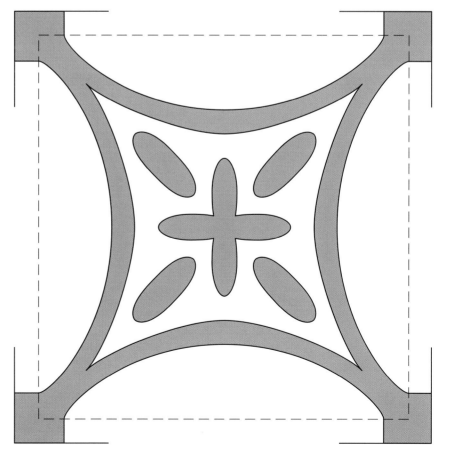

Tree of Life

Trellis

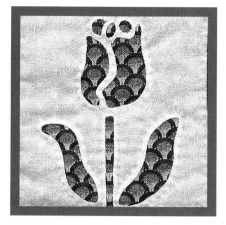

Tulip

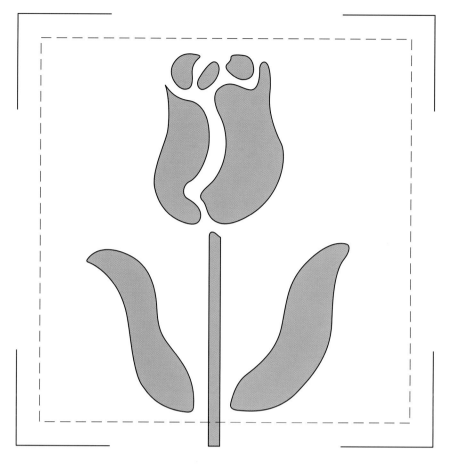

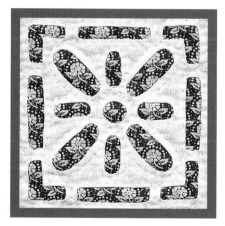

Twinkie

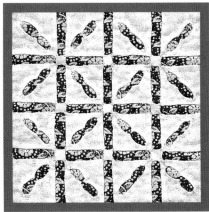

Twizzler

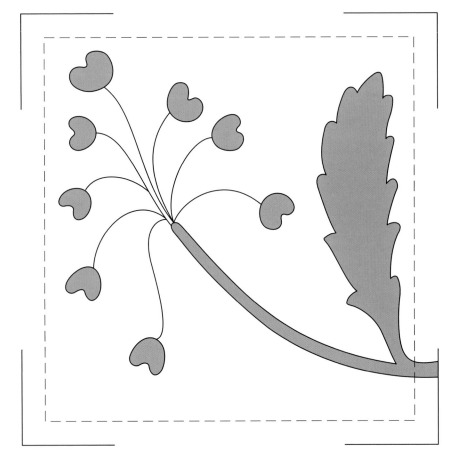

Undergrowth

Valentine

Violets

Waiting for Life

Wallpaper

Water Lily

Wheels on Fire

Windmill

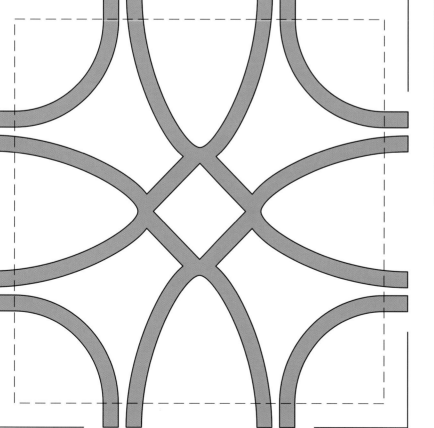

Window

Wooden Shoe

Wrought Iron

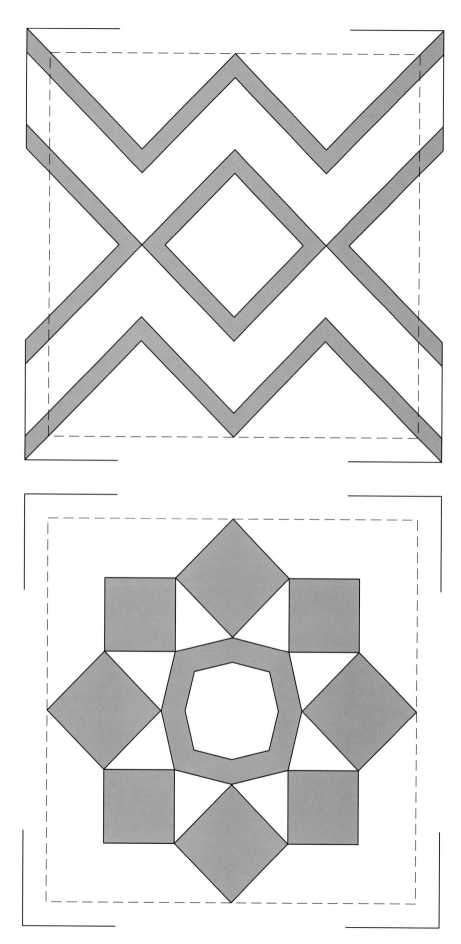

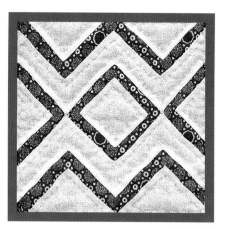

Zigzag

Zygote

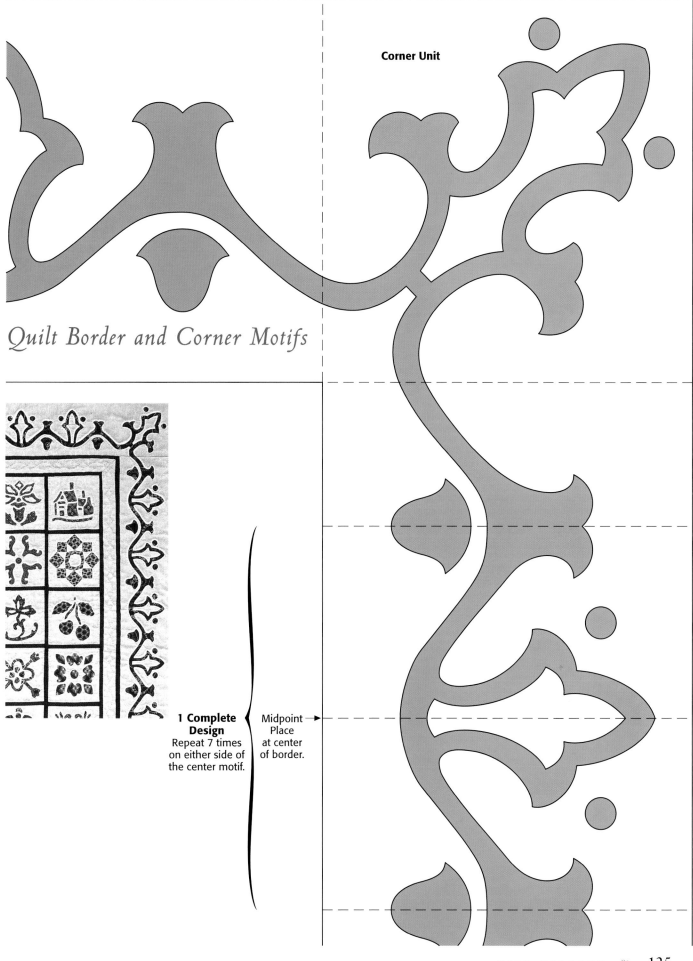

Corner Unit

Quilt Border and Corner Motifs

1 Complete Design
Repeat 7 times on either side of the center motif.

Midpoint →
Place at center of border.

Resources

IT IS ALWAYS a good idea to support your local quilt shop before shopping elsewhere. If you need to look further, these resources will be helpful.

The beautiful indigo fabrics in the "Deft Delft" quilt came from:
Cotton in the Cabin
Sandy McCay, Proprietor
17727 State Rd 1
Spencerville, IN 46788
260-238-4620
www.cottoninthecabin.com

Tiles available for purchase from:
Designs in Tile, Mount Shasta, CA
www.designsintile.com

Zsolnay Tile Museum
Newport, RI
www.drawrm.com/ztilemus.htm

Judy Garden's patterns available from:
www.patchworkgarden.com

Bibliography

Audsley, George Ashdown, and Maurice Ashdown Audsley. *Victorian Patterns and Designs in Full Color.* New York: Dover Publications, 1988.

Buckingham, Sandra Lynn. *Stencilling: a Harrowsmith Guide.* Camden East, Ontario: Camden House, 1989.

Buehl, Olivia Bell. *Tiles: Choosing, Designing, and Living with Ceramic Tile.* New York: Clarkson Potter, 1996.

Christie, Archibald H. *Pattern Design: An Introduction to the Study of Formal Ornament.* New York: Dover Publications, 1969.

Grafton, Carol Belanger, ed. *Floral Ornament.* New York: Dover Publications, 1997.

———. *Treasury of Japanese Designs and Motifs for Artists and Craftsmen.* New York: Dover Publications, 1983.

Hoppen, Stephanie, and Fritz von der Schulenberg. *Blue and White Living.* New York: Clarkson Potter, 1998.

Humbert, Claude, ed. *1000 Ornamental Designs for Artists and Craftspeople.* New York: Dover Publications, 2000.

Kasabian, Anna, with Julie Goodman. *Designing Interiors with Tile: Creative Ideas with Ceramic, Stone, and Mosaic.* Gloucester, MA: Rockport Publishers, Inc., 2000.

Menten, Theodore. *Ready-to-Use Decorative Corners.* New York: Dover Publications, 1987.

Typoni Inc. *Big Book of Graphic Designs and Devices.* New York: Dover Publications, 1990.

About the Author

Judy Garden was born in Holland and grew up in London, Ontario, Canada. She inherited her love for sewing from her mother, who made sure that Judy's hems and seams had accurate stitches (one reason Judy thought she would never be a quilter). It wasn't until her husband's career move brought their family to California that Judy discovered quilting was more than hand stitching. A sampler class quickly developed her love for quilting, which continued during a three-year stay in England. There she conducted her first trunk show in front of the village ladies, two cats, and a captured mouse. Judy continued to develop her talent for creating unique quilt designs throughout her years in England. Upon her return to Canada in 1994, she took a part-time job in a local quilt shop, where her passion for quilting blossomed into the founding of her own successful quilt pattern design company, The Patchwork Garden. Judy and her husband, Geoff, now live in Connecticut. They have three sons: Christopher, Matthew, and Alexander.